FAMOUS SHIPWRECKS

BY
DAVID & SUSAN SPENCE

Exploring the Deep

THE DIVING BARREL

An early and crude mechanically assisted piece of diving apparatus was Jacob Rowe's diving barrel, invented in 1753. The diver was encased in a hollow copper vessel with two holes for the occupant's arms to protrude and a glass view at one end. This enabled the diver to stay under the water for up to 30 minutes until all the air inside had been used up.

Ships have been wrecked for as long as man has put to sea. Some of the earliest evidence we have of ancient civilizations has come from wrecked ships. These are often time capsules carrying valuable information about the way the ships were built, the crew that sailed them and the passengers and cargoes they carried. This evidence enables researchers to build a vivid picture of the society of the time. Today sophisticated technology enables us to investigate deeper under the waves so that vessels, such as the *Titanic,* are beginning to yield their secrets.

THE DIVING BELL

The principle of the diving bell, which allowed man to be submerged but breathe air through a tube up to the surface, has been known and tried since at least the time of Aristotle (*c.* 350 BC). In the early 18th century Halley produced a crude diving bell made of wood coated in lead to make it heavy enough to sink. This was bell-shaped with a top of clear glass to provide light and a device to let out air expended by its user. The bell was reported to have been used at a depth of 18 metres (60 ft).

THE DIVING SUIT

A flexible suit was invented in 1797 by C.H. Klingert. It was made of tinplate and watertight leather and allowed the diver to walk around on the sea bed. Air was supplied through tubes from the ship above.

THE *ROYAL GEORGE* BELL

From 1834-6 the Deane brothers were to dive on the wreck of the *Royal George* using the copper-helmeted diving suit invented by John Deane. The story goes that whilst trying to save some horses from a fire, John Deane borrowed the helmet from a suit of armour. He secured to it the farm's failed water pipe and went into the smoke whilst a farmer slowly pumped air. Because of primitive diving techniques the most valuable items were salvaged first. These were the brass and iron guns and the ship's bell.

THE *ROYAL GEORGE* AT DOCK

The *Royal George* was 26 years old and the oldest 'first rate' ship in the service. On her last cruise the *Royal George* had been taking on water and was ordered in to dock. However, after a strict survey by experts, the leak was discovered and repaired, so docking was avoided. On 28 August it was noticed that the pipe delivering fresh water, which was situated just below the water line, was broken. It was in an effort to repair this pipe that caused her to sink.

A RUM DEAL

The most likely cause for her sinking started with a decision made by Admiral Kempenfelt to heel the ship to give access to the leaking fresh water pipe. When the men from the *Lark* unloaded tonnes of rum on the ship's low side, prior to stowing, she became so low that the slightest sea ripple entered the ship's lower gun-deck ports and gradually she began to sink. The carpenter, becoming aware of this, apparently twice asked the Lieutenant of the watch to right the ship. A sudden breeze blew and water rushed in to the lower ports. The workmen cried for the heeling to stop. The Lieutenant gave the order, but too late. The ship went down starboard side up, the water forcing out the air as she sank. Boats from the fleet, although quickly on the scene, were kept away by the whirlpool swirl. On touching the sea bed she settled with her masts nearly upright.

THE RAFT OF THE MEDUSA

Theodore Géricault was to paint his masterpiece based on the events of 1816. He painted 15 survivors and several trapped corpses afloat on the raft. Two of the survivors posed for the picture. It took 10 months to do the preliminary sketches and a further eight to make the painting. He never quite recovered from the despair he felt after completing this painting and in 1824 died after a long illness.

The painting was originally listed under another title: *Scene of Shipwreck*. This may have been because its true title was politically sensitive at a time when there was still much bad feeling between the Monarchists and the Republicans.

CANNIBALISM

Events on the raft quickly deteriorated. The men mutinied and fighting broke out. Some were killed before they expired from thirst and hunger, some committed suicide. With so much dead flesh, the survivors, forced by hunger, turned to cannibalism. Amazingly, after 52 days the wreck was finally discovered with four men still alive. A total of 155 people died.

RAFT AND BOATS

The plan was to abandon the ship and make for safety with the available boats, and to build a raft that would carry 200 men. The ship's boats would tow the raft (see diagram right). The raft however was badly panned and constructed (left). After three days the weather changed and the *Medusa* started to break up so the plan was put into action.

De Chaumery left with all the favoured Monarchist passengers in the boats along with their provisions. The raft could only manage about 160 people, consisting mainly of soldiers, who were submerged up to their waists in water. Their only provisions were six barrels of wine and two barrels of water. This left 60 or so people, including women and children, who could not fit on the raft and were abandoned on the sinking *Medusa*.

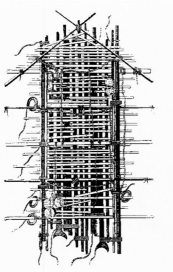

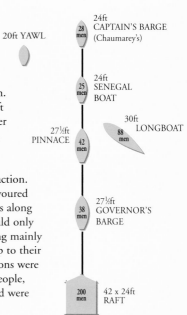

20ft YAWL

24ft CAPTAIN'S BARGE (Chaumarey's) — 28 men

24ft SENEGAL BOAT — 25 men

30ft LONGBOAT — 88 men

27½ft PINNACE — 42 men

27½ft GOVERNOR'S BARGE — 38 men

42 x 24ft RAFT — 200 men

The *Andrea Doria*

One of the biggest news stories of 1956 was the sinking of the *Andrea Doria*. The Italian luxury liner was sailing towards New York on 25 July 1956, carrying 1,706 passengers and crew on her 51st transatlantic crossing. The liner was due to make New York by 9 a.m. the following morning but she hit fog off the Nantucket coast and by evening visibility was reduced to under a kilometre. The Captain, Pietro Calamai, should have slowed the ship in such conditions but it appeared that he was anxious to make port on time because the ship's speed reduced only a fraction from the maximum 23 knots. Also making its way through the fog that night outward bound from New York was a passenger liner, the *Stockholm,* belonging to the Swedish American line. The *Stockholm* carried 747 passengers and crew. They were both headed on a fateful collision course.

ANDREA DORIA

The *Andrea Doria* was named after the 16th-century Italian Admiral depicted on this medal. His bronze statue adorned the first class lounge, and was the first artefact to be recovered by a salvage team in 1964.

S.O.S.

Mrs Dickson, a passenger on the *Andrea Doria,* was on the dance floor when the two ships collided. She recalls seeing a large shower of sparks and hearing shrieking metal, then the dance floor tilting at a crazy angle. Seawater rushed into the damaged starboard side causing the ship to list heavily.

There was an immediate scramble for the lifeboats as passengers attempted to save themselves. The *Stockholm* managed to secure watertight compartments and rescue passengers from the *Andrea Doria.*

The *Andrea Doria* slowly slipped under the waves as the first news reporters arrived, flying over the scene and giving an eye witness account of the ship's last moments.

COLLISION COURSE

10.40 p.m. The *Andrea Doria* picks up the *Stockholm* on its radar at a range of 27 km (17 miles).

10.50 p.m. The *Stockholm* changes course.

11.05 p.m. The *Andrea Doria* changes course. The ships are now closing on each other.

11.07 p.m. The *Stockholm* steers 20 degrees to starboard and the *Andrea Doria* takes emergency action, turning to port to avoid the other ship bearing down on her. The *Stockholm* turns to starboard in a final desperate avoiding action.

11.10 p.m. The reinforced ice-breaking bow of the *Stockholm* ploughs into the starboard side of the *Andrea Doria.* The damage is severe.

11.20 p.m. Captain Calamai sends the first S.O.S. message. He knows the *Andrea Doria* is doomed.

02.00 a.m. The liner *Ile de France* is the first ship to answer the S.O.S. and rescues 753 passengers.

05.30 a.m. The captain and senior officers are the last to leave the stricken vessel.

10.09 a.m. The *Andrea Doria* slips under the waves.

Environmental Disasters

SEA EMPRESS

The oil tanker *Sea Empress* ran aground in south-west Wales on 5 February 1996. Bad weather conditions made the ship's rescue all the more difficult and it is estimated that 72,000 tonnes of crude oil was lost. Eventually the ship was towed to Belfast. The clean-up operation was put into action very quickly.

Modern shipwrecks can have a disastrous effect on the marine environment. Today's supertankers carry thousands of tonnes of crude oil ready for refining into oil-based products such as petrol. Today, these dangers are seen to outweigh the threat posed to human life by sinking ships. Cargo ships, such as supertankers, often only carry a handful of crew and safety at sea is greatly improved thanks to such factors as accurate satellite navigation systems, the availability of detailed charts, and the sheer size of ships which are able to ride out rough weather. However when something goes wrong, it does so on a huge scale and human error is often to blame. Scientists have learned how to respond rapidly and effectively to disasters, such as oil spills, and are quickly able to minimize the damage that ensues.

THE *EXXON VALDEZ*

In 1989 the *Exxon Valdez* ran aground at Prince William Sound, in Alaska, dumping 267,000 barrels of oil (11 million gallons) over approximately 25,000 square kilometres (almost 10,000 square miles). Its effect on the ecosystem was severe and made more so because the accident happened in cold water. This prolongs the life of toxins and will affect wildlife species for generations. At the time it was the largest oil spill ever in the United States.

WILDLIFE IN DANGER

In the *Exxon Valdez* disaster, thousands
of seabirds, otters, fish and kelp were killed
as well as 16 whales and 147 bald eagles.

CLEAN-UP

The clean-up operation after the *Exxon Valdez*
disaster has been heavily criticized for its mismanagement as damaging
hydrocarbons were permitted to seep into the earth. The clean-up after
the *Sea Empress* disaster has been cited as one of the most successful,
many lessons having been learned from earlier oil spills. Oil was recovered
from the sea in sheltered areas and was taken to the open sea where it was
broken down with chemicals. The oil coating the beaches was treated with
high pressure hoses and scrapers. For the rocky areas they used absorbent
materials. The inaccessible areas were left to the natural cleaning power of the sea.

THE *AMOCO CADIZ*

During a storm in 1978, the American supertanker *Amoco
Cadiz,* filled with 223,000 tonnes of crude oil, ran aground off
the Brittany coast discharging its entire load into the Atlantic
Ocean. Some 130 beaches were coated in the oil and over
30,000 seabirds died along with millions of crabs, lobsters and
other fish, destroying the livelihoods of many local people.
Standard Oil of Indiana was found guilty of negligence
and failure to train the ship's crew. In 1988,
$85 million in damages was awarded
to the Breton communities (some
400,000 people) affected
by the disaster.

EXXON VALDEZ

Human Disasters

Tragedies at sea resulting in terrible loss of life are still commonplace today despite all the advances in ship technology and safety measures. Often human error is to blame, with either crew negligence or passenger ignorance resulting in disaster. Those that result in the loss of large numbers of people are ferry ships which often operate – and sink – in shallow coastal waters. Sometimes they occur in inland waters, such as the ferry MV *Bukoba*, which sank in Lake Victoria, Tanzania, in 1996 with huge loss of life. The ferry was heavily overcrowded, which may have been a factor in the capsizing. The following year about 180 passengers drowned when a Haitian ferry sank just a few hundred metres from shore. Again it was not known how many were on board, and an unknown number swam safely to shore.

THE *ESTONIA'S* LIFE RAFTS

Passengers of the *Estonia* struggled to get to the open decks as the ship rolled over. They scrambled onto the upturned hull where they were washed off by the waves. Within 50 minutes the ship sank. Only 137 passengers survived. Many were trapped and never made it into the 40 life rafts that floated, mostly empty, on the freezing seas.

THE *HERALD OF FREE ENTERPRISE*

On 6 March 1987 the *Herald of Free Enterprise* left Zeebrugge harbour in Belgium with approximately 500 passengers and 80 crew. Only 20 minutes into the journey and 2.5 km (1.5 miles) from shore the vessel capsized in freezing cold water. It took just 60 seconds to turn over. Eleven hundred tonnes of haulage, cars, and trucks shifted portside along with the passengers and anything that wasn't fastened down. There wasn't even time for a Mayday call. Nearly 200 lives were lost. A dredger saw the capsize and immediately raised the alarm, and within 30 minutes salvage ships, tugs and a helicopter were on the scene.

THE *ESTONIA* FERRY DISASTER

On 27 September 1994 the ferry *Estonia* sailed from Estonia to Stockholm carrying 989 passengers. About halfway into its journey across the Baltic, and in heavy seas with 6 metre (20 ft) high waves the ferry's huge steel bow door was torn from its hinges by the force of the sea (recovered later as shown). The ship listed to one side allowing seawater to pour into the lower decks. The crew, unsure as to what had happened, manoeuvred the *Estonia* sideways hoping the wind and waves would push her back onto an even keel. It had the opposite effect, allowing 20 tonnes of water per second to enter the stricken vessel.

THE *LUSITANIA*

It took just 18 minutes for the Lusitania *to sink.*

THE *SEA EMPRESS*

It is estimated that 72,000 tonnes of oil was lost.

THE *MARY ROSE*

Flagship of Henry VIII's fleet.

THE *ESTONIA* FERRY DISASTER

Sank en route to Stockholm.

THE *HERALD OF FREE ENTERPRISE*

Nearly 200 lives were lost.

THE *ROYAL GEORGE*

Sank off Spithead near Portsmouth.

THE *SERCE LIMANI*

Sank off the southern coast of Turkey.

THE *MEDUSA*

Theodore Géricault's masterpiece, The Raft of the Medusa.

THE *AMOCO CADIZ*

223,000 tonnes of crude oil was discharged into the Atlantic Ocean.

THE *RAINBOW WARRIOR*

French secret agents bomb and sink the Rainbow Warrior.

STORIES OF SURVIVAL

The wedding. The Indonesian ferry *Gurita* sank in a storm off the coast of Malaysia in January 1996. More than 150 people were lost but among the 47 survivors were Londoner Steve Nicholson, and his girlfriend Caroline Harrison. Harrison overcame her fear of the sea to take the ferry that night but was plunged into the sea as the ferry sank. Together they kept afloat for over 12 hours and, not knowing whether they would survive, steve proposed marriage and Caroline accepted.

Shark alert. New Yorker Margaret Crotty was also a passenger on the *Gurita*. When the ferry sank, Crotty jumped into the sea. She grabbed hold of a rubber life raft but was pushed off by passengers who feared it might capsize. Crotty removed her trousers, knotted the legs and trapped air into them creating a balloon that helped her stay afloat for 16 hours before finally reaching land. Her greatest fear was that she had cut her leg getting off the ferry and was afraid that hungry sharks might be attracted by the blood.

Saved by a bucket. In 1993 the ferry *Neptune* sank in a storm off the coast of Haiti. It was thought about 2,000 passengers were on board, of which only 285 survived. The captain, Benjamin St Clair, told how the passengers panicked when the ferry began to roll in the heavy seas, rushing from one side to the other. One survivor hugged a bag of charcoal for 15 hours after being swept into the sea. A woman survived by hanging onto a small white bucket. The ship carried no lifeboats, jackets, radios or other emergency equipment.

Heroic volunteers. The sailing ship *Heroine* foundered in a storm off the Dorset coast in 1852. Its fate could be seen from the nearby shore and five volunteers decided to row out to the stricken ship. Crowds cheered as they launched their boat but after a few minutes the boat was smashed back onto the breakwater and four of the five drowned. Meanwhile the crew and passengers of the *Heroine* were approaching shore in two of the ship's boats. A survivor swam ashore with a rope between his teeth and everyone was hauled to safety.

ACKNOWLEDGEMENTS

We would like to thank: Graham Rich, Rosalind Beckman and Elizabeth Wiggans for their assistance and David Hobbs for his map of the world.
Copyright © 2006 *ticktock* Entertainment Ltd., Great Britain.
First published in Great Britain 1997. All rights reserved.
No part of this publication may be reproduced, stored in a retrieval system, or transmitted in any form or by any means, electronic, mechanical, photocopying, recording or otherwise, without prior written permission of the copyright owner.
Printed in Hong Kong.

Picture Credits
t=top, b=bottom, c=centre, l=left, r=right, OFC=outside front cover, OBC=outside back cover, IFC=inside front cover

AKG; IFC, 5cr, 9br, 10tl, 11br, 12bl & 32ct, 17tr. Ann Ronan Picture Library; 2cl, 2cb, 2tl. Cephas Picture Library/Mick Rock; 15br. Chris Fairclough Colour Library; 14tl. Colorific; 2/3t, 8bl, 21tr, 21cr, 26/27 (main pic) & 30ct. Corbis; 24tl, 24bl, 24cr, 24br, 25c, 25tr & 30cl. Draeger Limited; 3br. e.t. archive; 13br, 18cl & OFC. FPG International; 22tl. Giraudon; 16/17t & 31bl. Glasgow Museums: The Stirling Maxwell Collection, Pollok House; 10/11b. Hulton Getty; 19c, 18/19c & OFC, 22/23c. Illustrated London News; 20bl. Institute of Nautical Archaeology; 6tl, 6bl & 31crb, 7tl, 6/7c, 7br. John Eaton and Charles Haas; 19br. Mary Evans Picture Library; 13tr, 22bl & OBC, 22/23t & 30tr & OBC, 23br. Mary Rose Trust; 8tl & 31ctr, 8br, 8/9c. National Maritime Museum; 11tr, 12/13c & 30tl & OFC, 14/15c, 14bl, 15tr & 31crc & OBC, 16cl, 18tl & 30bl, 20/21c. Planet Earth; OFC (diver), 2/3c, 5cb, 12tl & 30br & OFC. Rex Features; 4/5t, 26tl & 31ctl, 26/27ct, 27tr, 27cr & 31cb, 28cr & 31crt, 28tl, 28bl & 31tr, 28/29t & 31br, 29br. Spectrum Colour Library; 29cr. Telegraph Colour Library; 4b, 4tl, 9tr. The Kobal Collection; 20tl, 20ct. The Stock Market; 4/5 (main pic). Trustees of the National Museums and Galleries of Northern Ireland; 10bl & 30tr & OBC, 10c. Ulster Folk and Transport Museum; 19tr. Utopia Productions; 17br.

Every effort has been made to trace the copyright holders and we apologize in advance for any unintentional omissions.
We would be pleased to insert the appropriate acknowledgement in any subsequent edition of this publication.
A CIP Catalogue for this book is available from the British Library. ISBN 1 86007 460 X

snapping-turtle
guide